THE PERFECT CAREER

MAX A EGGERT
MA, BSc, AKC, FIPM, C.Psychol.

Max Eggert first read Theology before transferring his allegiance to Psychology and then to Industrial Relations.

He is managing partner of TRANSCAREER, an international consultancy dedicated to Human Resource Management and Outplacement. Many thousands of people at all levels and backgrounds have benefited their careers by working with Max who works in the UK and internationally as a strategist and as an adviser to organizations who retain his services.

Max has two children, and lives in London and Sussex. His passion is riding and his current interest is clinical hypnosis for career development.

OTHER TITLES IN THE SERIES

The Perfect Appraisal Howard Hudson
Perfect Assertiveness Jan Ferguson
The Perfect Business Plan Ron Johnson
The Perfect CV Max Eggert
Perfect Communications Andrew Leigh and Michael Maynard
The Perfect Conference Iain Maitland
The Perfect Consultant Max Eggert and Elaine van der Zeil
Perfect Counselling Max Eggert
Perfect Customer Care Ted Johns
Perfect Executive Health Dr Andrew Melhuish
Perfect Financial Ratios Terry Gasking
Perfect In-House Training Colin Jones-Evans
The Perfect Interview Max Eggert
The Perfect Leader Andrew Leigh and Michael Maynard
The Perfect Meeting David Sharman
The Perfect Negotiation Gavin Kennedy
Perfect People Skills Andrew Floyer Acland
The Perfect Presentation Andrew Leigh and Michael Maynard
Perfect Relaxation Elaine van der Zeil
Perfect Stress Control Carole McKenzie
Perfect Time Management Ted Johns

THE PERFECT CAREER

All you need to get it right first time

Max Eggert

RANDOM HOUSE
BUSINESS BOOKS

This edition published in the United Kingdom in 1999
by Random House Business Books

First published in 1994 by Arrow Books
Random House, 20 Vauxhall Bridge Road, London SW1V 2SA

Random House Australia (Pty) Limited
20 Alfred Street, Milsons Point
Sydney, New South Wales 2061, Australia

Random House New Zealand Limited
18 Poland Road, Glenfield
Auckland 10, New Zealand

Random House South Africa (Pty) Limited
Endulini, 5a Jubilee Road, Parktown 2193, South Africa

Random House UK Limited Reg. No. 954009

Papers used by Random House UK Limited are natural, recyclable products made from wood grown in sustainable forests. The manufacturing processes conform to the environmental regulations of the country of origin.

ISBN 0 09 940625 X

www.randomhouse.co.uk
businessbooks@randomhouse.co.uk

Typeset in Sabon by SX Composing DTP, Rayleigh, Essex
Printed and bound in Norway by AIT Trondheim AS

For
Heather Ann – about as
perfect as you can get

Feedback

Psychologists live off feedback. In life we all get it right by getting it wrong – we learn from our mistakes. If you have a comment about the contents, an observation or an addition then please write to me.

Send your feedback to:

Max A Eggert
c/o Random House Business Books
Random House
20 Vauxhall Bridge Road
London SW1V 2SA

THE QUOTATIONS

The American poet and essayist Emerson once wrote of quotations, 'By necessity, by proclivity – and by delight we all quote'. Quotations are sprinkled liberally in this little book because they capture the feel of what I am attempting to convey and unlock the truth more eloquently and succinctly than my clumsy words.

Sometimes the muse even visits psychologists and their families so I have been egotistical enough to quote myself, my father, and on one occasion my daughter Marisiân.

Contents

Section titles

Strategy

Acknowledgements

June Andrews – for brow-beating me into writing

Elizabeth Hennessy – for her patience in waiting for a very short script

Pauline Hyde – for pushing me into the first division

Val Lowman – for listening to this material over and over again

Fokkina McDonnell – for giving me the idea

David Parish – for holding the fort

Kathy Parkes – for typing and retyping

Heather Weatherstone – for giving me time and support

Introduction

Whilst I ply my trade as a management psychologist, the reader will not be surprised that most of this book comes from scar tissue from myself and others. You get things right by getting them wrong – however, in career terms that can be very expensive indeed. Because of the way careers work, it is of little value to yourself to look back on your career and reflect on what you should have done ten years ago.

I have listened to many captains of industry and those who live in the corridors of power in government agencies, both here and abroad, and many of their thoughts and reflections are presented in this little book. Typical of consultants (those that can't teach become consultants), there are no guarantees here except that it is possible to improve your lot with hard work, commitment and application. Success is about perspiration not inspiration. Those who have put into practice just a few of the suggestions contained here have become very successful indeed and claim they have 'Perfect Careers'.

I don't wish you luck because luck plays such a small part in achieving the perfect career. So I wish you every success.

Max A Eggert
Dunston,
Gateshead
September 1993

CHAPTER 1

Strategy

1. Stay mainstream 1

In pursuing your Perfect Career stay wherever you can in the mainstream. I am sure that the great restaurants in Paris have computer specialists working in them and that computer companies in California have chefs working for them. Now it is not impossible but highly unlikely that you will be a world famous chef working for Sun Microsystems or a leading edge computer specialist at George V, Paris, but I'm sure the point is obvious.

A manufacturing specialist is unlikely to be valued highly in a marketing driven firm or vice versa. Whatever your specialism, work in an organization where what you do is mainstream.

Find out which firms have the best reputation for your particular function or the area you wish to specialize in and then do your best to join them. Not only do you get the best training and the best experience, your career will benefit from their reputation.

2. Goals and targets

'Those who don't have personal goals will always be working for those who do.'

Max A Eggert

At a famous Business School on the first day of their studies students were asked which of them had written down quantifiable personal career goals. Surprisingly, for it was an ivy-league post-graduate school with a global reputation of producing the best, only three per cent of hands went up. Ten years later those three per cent were worth more in financial terms than all the other 97 per cent put together. Now whilst money is not everything, by and large it is not a bad indicator. The career message is clear.

Goals and targets turn dreams and visions of the future into reality. It is trite but right that if you don't know where you are going, anywhere will do. Goals and targets not only give you direction but help you to see the opportunities that others miss. Feeling hungry and driving through a new town you will be far more aware of food shops and restaurants. We look for what we want. If we only have vague ideas of what we want, we will not look for it and then opportunities will not be grasped as they occur.

Capitalism is a great system but it is also dangerous because if you do not have your own personal career objectives you will find yourself working to organizational objectives set down by others. Those who do not find this out early in life will never have a Perfect Career and unfortunately there are many who find out too late.

In most cases people think about their career objectives when they are about to finish their full time education and usually they are highly influenced by family or by school teachers who unfortunately do not always know as much as they should about the world of work or, most of all, about what is available in the local community. Often individuals just drift into any first job without seriously thinking through or being concerned about what sort of career may develop from their choice. Children often follow their parents and this is especially true of the professions.

In my days as a university recruiter I was always mildly surprised to discover that graduates frequently made their first job decisions based upon how much they liked the interviewers on the 'milk round' rather than on where a job in that firm would lead them. This is one of the main reasons why graduates do not stay with their first employer for very long. Many waste the first two years of their career sorting themselves out and in a career spanning 40 years that is a five per cent loss.

The other time when serious thought is allotted to personal career management is, unfortunately, when individuals lose their jobs through redundancy. This is a massive blow to the ego and it certainly makes people think about where their careers are going and who they are working for. Sometimes it takes redundancy for people to realize the hard lesson that the only person who is responsible for their security and their career is themselves.

Goals and targets need to be written down otherwise they stay as dreams and visions. Once goals are written down they take on a reality of their own and you begin to take them seriously. It is strange how at work we have all these skills and expertise (what project is ever submitted for approval without spelling out the objective?), but then do not apply such skills to our personal career situation. At work projects are always being defined and quantified so that they can be appraised. Even on an average manual salary in a lifetime you are likely to earn something approaching £750,000 at today's prices. The fact that you have invested in this book indicates that you will probably hope to earn far more. Now with a £750,000 project or investment don't you think it deserves some serious work on objectives, options and success criteria?

Objectives should be specific. It is not helpful to say 'I want to be famous' or 'I want to be rich' or 'I want to be great'. Everyone dreams this or something like it. Famous at what? Recognized by whom? Honoured in what way? It is not sufficient to be a 'Wannabe'. The more specific you are the more likely you are to be able to achieve the goal. Being specific forces your goals and targets to be less fanciful and more factual; they become more tied to reality; they become more obtainable and achievable.

Once the targets have been written down then it is possible to move on to the next stage which is giving them time frames. This then facilitates a timetable about what has to be done in terms of qualifications, experience and profile. Just like a management project, once the time objectives have been worked out then specific work schedules and resources can be allocated. You will have a programme for the year, the month, the week and even the day if necessary.

Some people have suggested that this takes all the fun and spontaneity out of life, that one becomes dominated by an impersonal system. This is simply not true. Targets just give you a focus but they can always be changed as your values or visions mature. What it does mean, however, is that with goals and targets which are specific and timebound, you will have far more control, far more options and thus far more freedom to do what you want to do with your life.

Alice: *Please sir, can you tell me the way?*
Cheshire Cat: *Where are you going?*
Alice: *I don't know.*
Cheshire Cat: *Then any road will take you there.*

Alice in Wonderland – Lewis Carroll

3. One shot

'To me old age is always 15 years older than I am.'
Bernard Baruch

There is no such thing as reincarnation in a career life, although I have met some chief executives who deserve to come back in the humblest capacity possible. In reality, if you don't get your career right first time you don't get sent back to 'Go' to start again and you certainly don't get £200.

Like it or not, we live in an ageist world with a golden decade of thirty–forty for men and, because this world is also sexist, for women it is twenty-five to thirty-five. This means that from the very outset of your career, you have a series of time windows which all begin to close slowly the moment you take your first job. If you aspire to a top position then you have to move as quickly as possible through the ranks otherwise you find that a window is closed blocking future opportunities. You only have to look at the job adverts in quality papers to see the number of age bands there are. Plot your career in job terms and then find similar jobs in the adverts and you can work out 'what you have to do by when' to get to where you want to go.

4. Make mistakes early

'If I had to live my life again, I'd make the same mistakes, only sooner.'
Tallulah Bankhead

We get things right by getting them wrong. In career terms you cannot make a mistake, you can only give yourself a 'learning opportunity'.

However, it is best to make all your career mistakes earlier rather than later. As your career develops and you move up the corporate ladder, recovery time is extended. Your career is like your body in that the older you are, the longer it takes for bruises to heal and bones to mend.

Most successful people make one major career error but they do it early and they learn from it.

5. Stay mainstream 2

Stay as long as you can in mainstream companies which are in the *Times* Top 100 or Fortune 500. These firms have the reputation and the career equivalent of street credibility. They are the Eton and Harrow of work, the Oxford and Cambridge of careers.

Once you move out from the mainstream into a lesser tributary, your chances of getting back into the swim are minimal. There is always a best and it is worthwhile shooting for it. If you are going to take your career seriously it is worthwhile shooting for the gold bullseye on the target. There is no guarantee that you will get the centre every time but your score rate will be that much higher than if you just aim loosely in the direction of the target, hoping for success.

Because you are successful (and you must be since you have had blue chip experience) you will be very attractive to smaller firms. Take heed, though, this is very much a one way ticket. Once you have left the first division it is difficult to get back. If you have left a blue chip firm for a second division one the reverse trip is difficult as any footballer will tell you.

'*Experience is the child of thought, and thought is the child of action.*'

Benjamin Disraeli

6. Deal with what you can touch

'All experience is an arch, to build upon.'

Henry Adams

At one time I helped run a small electronics firm at a time when the Pound was getting weaker against the Dollar all the time. Since the firm was American this caused great concern because no matter how efficient the plant was, how hard we worked, how good we were, there was no way that we were going to make the product levels expected of us when our sterling profits were consolidated into dollars.

For a long time we had meeting after meeting to discuss what we could do about the situation until it suddenly dawned on me that there was nothing I could do, nor could the team, nor could anyone – if the Pound dropped through the floor all that we could do was run the most efficient factory possible. No amount of discussion concerning the currency was going to change the situation. In fact, such discussions were a waste of good management time. All we could do was manage what we could touch and that meant having the best production facility run by the best people we could get.

It was an important lesson. I understand that great tennis players don't worry about winning Wimbledon, winning the match, the set or even the game – when under pressure they just concentrate on getting the ball over the net successfully. Just keep doing the best you can with what you have got and you will be successful – not just in the short term but in the long term as well.

When we think about our career we worry a lot about what we should have done or what has happened or, alternatively, we worry about the future and what might happen. All of these are inappropriate behaviours. The past helps you learn from your mistakes and the thinking about the future provides opportunities to anticipate difficulties, but that is all. What you need to do is concentrate on the most important work you should be doing today.

'Jumping at several small opportunities may get us there more quickly than waiting for one big one to come along.'
Hugh Allen

7. Two types of pay

'There is no security in this life. There is only opportunity.'
Douglas MacArthur

Rewards in organizations come in two forms, one obvious in the form of pay and the other more subtle – namely, experience. Both are valuable in their own way but pay in the form of experience is accumulative and, what's more, it is difficult to lose once you have gained it. You can't have an overdraft of experience.

It is usually thought that qualifications are the key for success but this is not so. Only about 15 per cent of managers and executives are qualified for what they do; the other 85 per cent have experience. Qualifications are, of course, important but they only determine how high up the ladder you start (and no one starts at the top!) but it is experience that takes you most of the way in your career. I train hundreds of people every year in how to be interviewed. Not one of them has ever come back from an interview and said they were asked about what class of degree they got, but they all report being asked lots of questions about their experience.

The message is clear – treat experience as seriously as you do your salary. It is strange that employees ask for pay rises and work hard to achieve a bonus but so few ask for the sort of experience they need for their career.

Sometimes employees almost make the ultimate career sacrifice. They stay locked into a boring, dead-end job for years because of the money and all the time their real value in career terms, that is their experience, is continually being devalued.

Take your experience seriously, work hard for it, negotiate for it because it is a key to your perfect career.

'*A wise man will make more opportunities than he finds.*'

Francis Bacon

8. What's next?

I'm always interested in how people got the jobs they do and am frequently amazed when in answer to the question 'How did you do it?' they just say 'I was offered it.'!! It is as if people are in career drift, in that they accept jobs on the basis that they are offered to them.

Would you start travelling in a certain direction unless it took you where you wanted to go? Would you go into a shop which did not offer what you wanted to buy? Of course not – but it is surprising that people are so flattered to be offered a position that they take it without thinking 'where does it lead – what's next?' Five years down the track they discover themselves sidelined into jobs they do not like or enjoy and which are very difficult to move out of. There is a lovely story about two men travelling down the motorway and one says to the other, 'Where are we going?', only to get the reply 'I don't know, but we're making great time!'

Most employers are not going to give you jobs for the sake of your career development but really to meet pressing and urgent organizational requirements. The first allegiance of the organization is to its owners, then to its customers, next its product or service and finally to its employees. Make sure that you work to fulfil your own objectives rather than those of others. It is legitimate to work for yourself.

'I am not in Wall Street for my health.'
J P Morgan

9. Pick your boss

Your boss is key to your future so make sure whenever you can that you have a good one, not only in the sense that you will be managed well but also that his or her standing in the organization matches your career aspirations.

You might be brilliant but if your boss is naff then your brilliance will be considerably dulled.

If you can get someone who is a rising star, then,

- you will learn and develop more quickly
- when they are promoted you have a good chance of getting their job
- the boss might take you up with the promotion
- you gain another friend in high places
- if the boss fails in the new job then it is obvious who made him or her a success

So, when considering the job, questions to ask could include some of the following:

- How long has the boss been in the job?
- What is his/her standing in the organization?
- Is he/she well respected?
- Is he/she in line for promotion in the near to medium future?

- How well connected is my boss within the organization?
- How does my boss see his/her career developing?
- Is my boss still achieving in the job?
- Has my boss reached his/her peak in career terms?

If you want to be a rising star then work with the brightest star you can. If your boss is not going places, chances are you won't either.

10. Seeing is believing

Many would be forgiven for thinking that if they work hard then they will be rewarded. Well, this is true to a certain extent – of course it does take hard work to succeed but it also has to be seen and appreciated by those who count. You could be the hardest working person in the organization but if those who should know about it don't, then you won't get the recognition. You need to achieve profile for what you are doing to secure the perfect career.

Before taking on a task, project or job, just ask yourself how much profile is it going to give you with those who hold the keys to your future, and if the answer is 'Not much' then think twice before moving or undertaking the project.

At one time I used to do a lot of work with middle management at Goodyear Tyre and Rubber Company which had an excellent reputation for promotion from within. Many of the managers gained their first step on the ladder of their careers either by putting themselves forward as a shop steward or as a safety representative. These positions gave them profile, as individuals they were seen by the people that counted – those who could promote them. It is a concept politicians use much of the time. There are many social issues which deserve attention but some enjoy far more media appeal than others and you can guess which ones will have more attention.

Who are the people who are known in your organization and how do they manage to get promotion – in both senses of the word?!

'*Ability without visibility is a disability.*'
Max A Eggert

11. Take charge 1

You are responsible for yourself and your career; no one else is. Employers want you primarily for your current skills and the expertise you have to date; it is essentially a commercial relationship with certainly no obligation to provide you with total job security or developmental experience, let alone a career.

So take charge of yourself. Do not wait for an appraisal or a formal management development opportunity to be offered to you. Get on with your own career development. If you happen to work for an organization with an effective management development scheme based on appraisal, that is a bonus, but don't count on it. Most perfect careers are based on the 'Do it Yourself' philosophy. It is the difference between being reactive and proactive.

'*Destiny is not a matter of chance, it is a matter of choice.*'
William Jennings Bryan

12. Take charge 2

'*Seek and you will find. Ask and it will be given to you.*'
Jesus Christ

It is a mistake to wait to be told what the limits of your

authority are. In organizations the more authority you have, the more power you have and the more you can create an environment and the jobs for the perfect career.

When playing rugby a fellow team member of mine would deliberately break every rule in the book in the first ten minutes of the game. The reason was simple – he then knew how the referee worked and what was possible and what was not. A simple strategy which gave our team a distinct advantage.

When you gain a new position push the boundaries of your power as soon as you can to ensure that you then know how to play the management game right from the start.

13. Failure goes with trying but so does success

'*To avoid criticism, do nothing, say nothing, be nothing.*'

Elbert Hubbard

Success is about taking risks and taking risks means that you are not going to win every time. But if you don't try you are definitely not going to be successful.

Realism is important in all that you attempt. No matter how well prepared you are, or how hard you work you will

- not always get the job you want or the promotion you deserve
- be beaten by others better than you
- be in the wrong place at the right time and vice versa
- be adversely affected by market and technology changes beyond your control
- still perform badly occasionally and have off days
- not achieve continuous success

All these things occur with trying. Failure is not falling down, it is refusing to get up again. It is platitudinous but if you don't buy the ticket you don't get in the game, and if you don't play you won't win. Showing up and giving of your best is the greater part of success. Take every opportunity to be there, to try, to develop and to grow. Most things in life take skill derived from experience and practice. You are not expected to get everything right each time. Obviously you can't be like the person whose appraisal read: 'He only makes mistakes once but he seems to make an awful lot of them,' but the message is clear for careers – if someone gives you an opportunity or you create one for yourself, then 'just do it'.

'People pretend not to like grapes when they are too high for them to reach.'
Marguerite de Navarre

14. Get known for skills sets
One of the rules about promotion is: DON'T BE GOOD AT YOUR JOB, BE GOOD AT THE SKILLS NEEDED FOR YOUR JOB.

Sometimes people who are really good at their job make themselves indispensable and then their manager blocks their promotion. A regional sales manager, for instance, is not likely to want his best sales person to move to a regional sales manager position elsewhere. Not only does he lose his best sales person, but he also has another career competitor. You have to remember that your manager's career depends on your performance, not on how good he is in providing training or bringing on future managers. It is obvious that the reason why some managers do not endorse the promotion of their best performers is simply because it might adversely affect their own performance and thus their own career prospects.

A way out of this difficulty is to build a reputation around skill sets such as – good with people, good at negotiation, technically brilliant, creative, etc. Demonstrate how good your skills are in the job but do not make yourself indispensable. In this way you do not become limited by your job title but continually demonstrate the skill required for your present and next position.

'If you feel you are indispensable, put your head in a bucket of water, withdraw it, and contemplate the size of the hole you have left.'

David Charles Evans

15. Don't stay to enjoy your successes

Most people stay in jobs for too long and never reach their full potential. The Peter Principle is correct – 'People rise to the level of their incompetence' – but there is the Max corollary – 'Most incompetence at work is caused by boredom not through lack of ability.'

In the fast food trade the preferred customers are those who 'get, gobble and go'. They are preferred because they spend their money, consume the product and make room for others to do the same. You should have the same attitude to the job – get, gobble and go. Give the job your very best, learn as much as you can, contribute as much as you can and when both these things are done it is then time to move on. Do not stay to enjoy your success.

Young, successful people in organizations are called 'comers' because they are coming through. No employer today can offer you job security, only experience. You in return give the best you can but when you have done the job to the best of your ability and you are at the peak performance then it is time for you to move on should you choose to. In this way everybody wins. You gain new opportunities and experience, the employer can exercise an active promotion policy and someone else gets a shot at your old job.

If you are at peak performance and you stay to enjoy your success, then being at the top there is only one way to go and that is down. When you go off the boil and no longer have the zeal you once had, it is unlikely that you are going to be high up in the promotion candidature stakes.

We can call this 'career scalloping' (see the figure below) – keep going up the organization or your profession until you decide that where you are is where you want to stay. Use your successes and achievements to promote yourself not to lock yourself in. Do not become a victim of your own success.

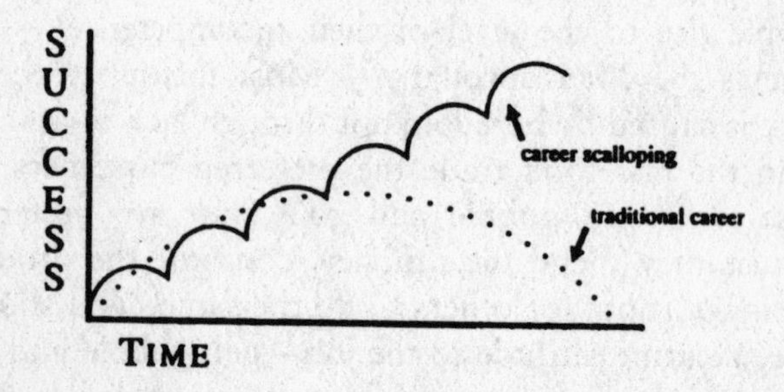

Here are some questions to help you decide whether you should think about moving on:

- Do you find yourself getting bored at work?
- Can you solve 90 per cent of the problems quickly with a feeling of 'here we go again'?
- Do you find yourself with time on your hands?

- Do you feel that your contribution to the success of the organization is not as great as it used to be?
- Do you envy other people in their jobs?
- Do you frequently get the feeling that others must have better jobs than you?
- Do you get the impression that you are seriously underpaid or that your working conditions are not as good as they should be?
- Have you been in the job for a longer period than the person who held it before you?

If the answer is 'Yes' to any of these questions, then it is time to think about scalloping upwards.

'*To become what we are capable of, becoming is the only end in life.*'
Robert Louis Stevenson

16. The organizational man

'*Either do as your neighbours do or move away.*'
Moroccan Proverb

Organizations are not all that different from people in that what they say and what they do are sometimes very different. How often have you heard the chief executive of a family say to the five-year-old and youngest team member, 'Don't do what I do, do as I say'? So the way to discover what is really required of you by organizations or by individuals is by looking at what they do.

Sometimes organizations send strong PR and public messages contained in mission statements, policy statements and even job descriptions but what is actually required from you is something different. A simple way through this, especially when first joining an organization, is to ask yourself a set of basic questions:

- Who around here is the organization man?
- Who around here appears to be a rising star?
- Who is well plugged into the systems and values here?
- Who is used as a role model?

The easy bit is to ask yourself:

- What do they do?
- How do they do their work?
- How do they behave?
- What do they give priorities to?
- What are their values?

Then the hard part is asking yourself:

- How am I different from them and what do I wish to do about the difference between us?

Hard because either you are going to have to change your behaviour or you are going to have to change your job. If you do not change you will not get on nor, more importantly, will you be happy now you have discovered what is really required of you. If you do not fit your performance will be dulled and your disappointment will show.

'*It is easier to move to a new job today than it is tomorrow.*'

Max A Eggert

17. The brigadier and the general

I once was involved with an MOD contract, assisting senior officers in the armed services into civvy street if they retired early. It was one of the most enjoyable and rewarding contracts I ever had, working with such high calibre and competent people.

We worked in groups and in one group I worked with a brigadier. I usually started my counselling sessions with the question 'How did you get to be where you are?' The question broke the ice and helped me to get to know my client quickly. However, the brigadier replied, 'Well, if I had been as lucky as Sir Peter – over there, I would have made general as he did. He saw active service early, got a good staff job, worked for NATO and in Northern Ireland. He was really fortunate in his postings and tours.'

Later, I worked with the general and asked the same question, 'How did you get to where you are?' 'Well,' replied Sir Peter, 'I always wanted to do well and I knew that there was early promotion to be gained in active service so I went to Aden. Then it was imperative for me to get a strategy job so I managed to gain an MOD post. After that I had to have my BTA (Been To America) so I used all my networking skills to get a job in Washington.'

Both were able men in terms of ability, intelligence and interpersonal skills, but the difference between the two was vision and firm goals.

'*He who can see three days ahead will be rich, for three thousand years.*'

Shigariro Unno

18. Which jobs are for comers?

If you are in a large organization look up the career histories of those at the top. Track back the positions they held. Which divisions did they work in, which functions? Usually there are patterns and themes and specific jobs which are known as slots for up and coming fast track employees (comers). It does not matter whether it is a particular product sales manager position in a pharmaceutical giant, a production job in a car manufacturer, assistant to the Chairman in retailing, or a particular parish in the Church of England, each post is known to springboard 'comers' to their next stage.

Position yourself as best you can for those jobs. If you can't do that, then plan B should be to get as close to those jobs as you can so that at least you will be in the network of the 'comers' as they move through.

If this stretches your credulity, go and discover what happens to

National sales managers at SKB
Plant managers at Jaguar
Assistants to the Chairman at M&S
Vicars and curates from St Stephen's, Rochester Row

19. Use meetings

Most people sensibly do not have meetings because they take up so much time which could be profitably spent doing the job.

But meetings do provide an ideal opportunity to increase your profile. Every meeting has an agenda but when you attend you should develop you own covert career agenda which will include such questions as:

How can I use this meeting to:

- let people know what I'm doing?
- gain resources for myself?
- impress people?
- form allies and allegiances?
- learn?
- find out what interpersonal skills I can develop?
- observe what people want and how they attempt to get it?

When you use meetings as opportunities to promote yourself, your work and/or as learning laboratories you will find that they are always worthwhile and interesting.

20. Be a rodent

Certain rodents enjoy a reputation for acting very sensibly when a ship starts taking in too much water – they leave. Remember that on the *Titanic* even the best officers went down too, so unless your firm gives great separation packages (the corporate equivalent of lifeboats), and fewer and fewer do, leave early. Is this selfish? Yes, it is, but my experience of firms is that when times are hard they become ruthless. Your career needs you not only to be successful but also to grow in a successful environment with a reputation that goes with it.

What sort of statement are you making about your own performance if you are a senior executive in a firm that goes down? Were you not in some way responsible for your own demise?

Here are some signs that sensible rodents watch for:

- Managers have more time for themselves than they do for their subordinates.
- Promised equipment is always delayed or postponed indefinitely.
- Good cost saving ideas requiring an initial investment are not implemented.
- Top managers come and go quickly.
- Head count is frozen and shrinks.
- Important equipment is moved out to other sites.
- Staff who make long term contributions are not replaced or are transferred, e.g. people from marketing, research, training.
- Production lines are not run at full speed.

- Absenteeism is not controlled as well as it used to be.
- Senior HQ staff and senior visitors are seen more frequently. Smartly dressed people whom you do not recognize are more in evidence.
- One reorganization is not given time to settle down before another is initiated.
- Planned maintenance is reduced or run down significantly.

CHAPTER 2

Working with others

21. Work for your boss

On Brighton Pier along with all the summertime paraphernalia of holiday souvenirs, candy floss and rock, you used to be able to get a brass plaque that said:

> Rule 1: The Boss is always right
> Rule 2: If the Boss is wrong, see Rule 1

and it was strange to discover such a basic career truth hidden away with all the nonsense of holiday tat and bric-a-brac. It is well to remember that the only way to the top is by being promoted and the key to promotion is your boss.

So often in our work we get caught doing things we think we should be doing or because someone in Human Resources wrote it in a job description some time ago.

In Management, things go in phases of popularity; they wax and wane. Sometimes job descriptions and lists of accountabilities have their turn at being popular. The difficulty with job accountabilities is that their value is limited to the time they were written. They are like sets of accounts which give a snapshot of the financial position in any one year. Organizations are not static – they constantly change – and you could easily find yourself working to the wrong or inappropriate set of instructions. Rather like turning up at a railway station with an old timetable – you become out of tune with the rest of the organization and your boss in particular.

Like the popularity of job descriptions, some organizations have mission statements. Now these are very helpful if they are owned by the whole of the organization but frequently they are lifted from somewhere else by the board of directors whilst off on a management junket. Mission statements get delivered like the ten commandments of Sinai but with no explanation or training or commitment, let alone a Moses and Aaron to see they are implemented. Woe betide you if you try and work to mission statements if your boss does not share and work to them as well.

Your boss is the key to your success. If he or she does well then you will do well. Abandon job descriptions, mission statement instructions from the management development department and just ask yourself:

- What does my boss want me to do?
- What at work is important to my boss?
- How can I help my boss most?
- What does my boss get concerned about?
- When is my boss pleased about my work or the work of others and why?

And you will find that not only do you save yourself a lot of time but your boss's boss also begins to notice you because everyone wants a good, loyal performer working for them.

22. Network

'*I get by with a little help from my friends.*'
The Beatles

Networking is a very popular concept today but it has always existed. There is that popular phrase 'It is not what you know, but who you know that counts.'

It has to be remembered that as humans we have spent more time in tribes fighting and eating one another than we have working in corporations or living in semi-detached houses. Being members of the same tribe is very important in terms of absolute survival and there are still strong vestiges of this instinct today. We have cavemen instincts in twentieth-century corporations.

It is very normal if not natural to do favours for and make exceptions for our friends as opposed to strangers. All things being equal, I will give a friend a job, help, advice, support and information just because they are my friend.

This is not a new thing. In ancient times letters of introduction were given to travellers to new places. Ever since Adam came out of the Garden of Eden we started networking and so did Eve. Mutual support in primitive societies is exceptionally strong. Today networking is sometimes formalized, as in the Freemasons, and sometimes it is woven into a social structure such as the Round Table or more formalized as in the CBI or TUC.

Assisting executives as I do in my work as Career Counsellor, I know that something like 40 per cent of jobs are not gained through employment agencies or job adverts but through networking. As a consultant most of my work does not come from advertising – in fact we don't advertise at all – but from networking. I have to make it my business to know people. People make it their business to know me. At some time we are going to need each other. Achieving the Perfect Career is a two-way street – you help others when and where you can and they at some time in the future may be able to help you. It is not only monkeys that scratch each other.

In the eighties there used to be a sticker in the back of fast motor cars sported by young men in red braces which said 'The person with the most toys wins'. In the tough nineties it should read 'The person with the largest network wins'.

To develop and keep control of your network you should have a set of 5″ x 3″ postcards and on them keep information on the people you meet in a work or social context who might be able to help you. Besides the usual things like name, address and telephone number, include other things like job, experience, skills, and the occasional personal detail – children, interests, favourite drink, etc.

Networks are like plants, they need cultivating. You can't meet someone at a seminar and then five years later ring them up and expect them to remember you, even less help you with your career. Relationships take time. Keep in touch with cards and update sheets on yourself, clippings of articles you think they will find interesting. Agree to meet for dinner or lunch when you are in their area. Exchange useful information for each other. When a network colleague has a difficulty, think who in your network might be able to help and put them together.

Questions people ask themselves in organizations are different at different levels. When having to do something difficult people on the lowest rung ask themselves 'How am I going to do this?' and at the highest level the question becomes 'Who do I know who has encountered this problem before?' The higher you go, the more important networking becomes.

The jockey that wins is usually the one with the best

horse for support – the Perfect Career usually goes to the one with the best network for support.

Start networking – now!

'*A faithful friend is the medicine of life.*'

Ecclesiasticus 6.16

23. Don't share your long-term ambitions

It is a sad fact of life but it is true – most people want you to be successful but not more successful than they are.

So you would be wise to be cautious and keep your long-term hopes very private. I am not too close to cabinet ministers but none of them goes round saying they want to be Prime Minister. Politicians in America make a real thing about not declaring their nomination for the Presidency. You are not going to get very far – even past the interview – if you express to other aspirants that you wish to be Executive Vice President Western Hemisphere. Bubbles can appear over the heads of recruiters or bosses which say 'over my dead body' or 'get in line'.

All you should do is express a desire to do your present job well and be confident that opportunities will open up for you. If you are quite clear about your career objectives (see section 2) opportunities will occur and you will be in an ideal position to grasp them.

24. Get advice but be selective

'*Advice is what we ask for when we already know the answer but wish we didn't.*'

Erica Jong

I never mind about giving advice for the proclivity to give it is matched by an equal proclivity to ignore it.

Everyone will give you advice and that is useful but you have to be selective. Professionals in one sphere are not necessarily experts in another but some will have wisdom born of intelligence and experience.

It is said that poor people should take rich people out to lunch for that is the way to learn. Some career advisers suggest that you should appoint your own non-executive board of career advisers – mentors whose views you value and who are further along their career paths than you are. The view higher up the mountain is not only more beautiful, it is usually much more clear and you can see further. Those who are higher up can be of great help in getting your career plans and difficulties into perspective.

Seek out those who have got there before you, have gone where you want to go, and ask them how they did it, what they would have done differently – a polite way of asking what mistakes they made – and if they would mind talking to you once every six months or so. Most executives in the latter part of their careers enjoy and almost have a need to tell others about their achievements and how they were won. It was once said that those that don't take note of history have to relive it. You will make enough mistakes in your career anyway, everyone does, so why not avoid the more obvious ones by getting good quality advice from people who have done it?

'*America's best buy for a nickel is a telephone call to the right man.*'

Iika Chase

CHAPTER 3

Working with self

25. Be personally responsible

'No bird soars too high, if he soars with his own wings.'

William Blake

Sometimes I get invited to talk at universities or business schools to graduate and mature students and I have great fun asking them who is or who will be responsible for their management training and development. Usually there are a whole lot of responses including the Training Officer, the Graduate Trainer, the Management Development people. Sometimes we get a more enlightened response such as 'my manager'. I then ask questions about the expertise and efficacy of these employees. 'How good are they in looking after your specific needs?' I ask. This brings the same sort of response as 'what do you think of British Rail catering?'.

And then the coup de grâce. 'And you let them be responsible for your future?' This does not make me popular with the students but it brings home the point very forcefully about personal responsibility for one's own training and development. With a little bit of work and forethought you are in the best position to be your own management development manager. Why wait for your company to train you or organize your experience? Why can't you do it for yourself? If you are not interested in your own training, why should anyone else be?

Personal responsibility is a constant theme in this little book which keeps popping up in a number of guises. You have to take charge of your career – if you leave it to your organization, you will find yourself marching to a drum which is not your own.

Self Responsibility means

- being honest with yourself about your skills and abilities, likes and dislikes, hopes and fears.
- being disciplined in working on yourself and what you need to do to get where you are going.
- being realistic about what is and what is not possible to achieve in the short term.
- being persistent and focused about what you want and not being dissuaded by failure or by the inappropriate comments of others.
- being proactive in your environment rather than waiting for things to come your way or for luck to deal you in.
- being self assertive in making choices and taking reasonable risks with people and opportunities and accepting the outcomes of those risks.

Spend money on your own development. How much is up to you but I would suggest not less than you spend on business clothes and dress each year. Strange how we can spend all that money decorating our bodies and yet next to nothing on feeding our minds or developing our skills.

What is to stop you putting yourself on a course or a

programme or even organizing a learning set at work with like-minded people. In a self-learning set you select who you want to work with, how long you want to work and what topics you want to work on.

When I illustrate this point with executives or on my management programme I ask people 'How many of you rent a car for business?' and, being executives, most hands go up. Then I ask 'How many of you clean and valet the cars you hire?' and most of the hands stay down. What is the difference? It is about ownership. If you own something you take an interest in it and look after it. Take an interest in your own career and own it.

26. Self reward

A great emphasis in this book is placed on doing things for yourself and the reason for this is obvious – no one else is as committed to your success as you should be. Here is a potential area of difficulty – if no one else is interested in your career you might not try. Motivation theory teaches us that much of what we do is to win esteem, or earn recognition from others or from institutions. Napoleon was supposed to have remarked: 'I have made a great discovery: men will die for stripes of coloured ribbon.' It is not uncommon for us to work harder for others than we would for ourselves.

If you are going to work for your own career then some thought has to be given as to how you are going to reward yourself, especially for the 101 small, tedious things that need to be done along the way. Big outcomes, like achieving the new job, the promotion or the qualification will bring their own obvious reward and recognition but what about all the little steps along the way?

When I work with job searchers we decide firstly on

how each major section of this process will be recognized and rewarded. Usually the following are the major steps in the process:

- The Self Review
- The CV
- The First Interview
- The First 100 Polite Turn Downs
- The First Offer
- Accepting the new job

All of these are major elements of the job search process and need to be recognized and rewarded in a significant individual and meaningful way.

Psychologists tell us:

- What gets asked for gets done
- What gets measured gets done better
- What gets rewarded gets done best of all

So for your career the implications are obvious –

- Set yourself targets
- Make them quantifiable and time bound
- Reward yourself for their achievement

These rewards need not be big. I know someone who treats himself to salt and vinegar crisps and chocolate bars when he achieves a small goal; a film for something more significant; a silk tie for a minor success, and an expensive suit or a foreign trip for a major life goal.

'If I had served my God as I have served my king, I would not be going to the place I am going now.'

Cardinal Wolsey on his death bed

27. Stick with your strong points

'Everyone has talent. What is rare is the courage to follow the talent to the dark places where it leads.'
Erica Jong

You don't have to be perfect to have a Perfect Career, in fact it is impossible. No one is perfect, no one is good at everything. At school we are trained to work hard and improve where we are weak. We have to do things again and again until we get them right but in careers a different approach is required. It is not, however, always easy to change the habits one learnt at school.

The advice is do not worry too much about your weaknesses but always play to your strengths. Whenever you can, make sure you have a subordinate or a colleague who is good at those things you are not so hot on. You don't have a dog and bark yourself so if you are weak on details get someone who is strong on the small things. If you are more of a private person team up with a front man who enjoys doing all that high profile stuff. If you are a strategist, get a tactics person, and vice versa.

The higher up the management tree, the easier it is to build round you the elements of the perfect team for you. This means that you can always play to your strengths and look as if you are perfect.

Ned Seagoon: 'Yes, but who are you?'
Eccles: 'Oh, the hard ones first, eh!'
The Goons

28. Interpersonal skills

One of the many things that is interesting about organizations is that the criteria for success continually change the higher up the ladder you go. On the lower rungs of the organization the emphasis is upon technical and professional competence – being able to do things well and get things done. If you are good at this then your promotion is almost assured.

On the next level, that of management, technical competence is still important but interpersonal skills begin to take on a greater significance. Once you start being responsible for other people, interpersonal skills including those of persuasion, motivation and negotiation grow in significance. What is important here is the skill and ability to get other people as well as your peers to do things well for you. You can be technically superb as a manager but your success depends on getting the technical best out of your subordinates and winning the support and resources from your bosses and colleagues so that your people can perform well for you.

At this stage in your career you are rather like a player-manager. You get on the pitch regularly and practise your technical skills but you have to get the best out of your team.

At the next stage interpersonal skills are important but on the inside track and coming up fast are strategic skills. Being able to see further than anyone else. Being able to appreciate the implications of various options and decisions. Being able to read the situation before it occurs. You just cannot do this if you are tied down to the technology or you are still on the playing field. The view is more comprehensive from the Director's Box.

People who run large organizations well can run anything well. It does not matter if it is Pepsi Cola or Apple Computers, Amstrad or Tottenham Hotspur. Cabinet Ministers can be Home Secretary one day and Chancellor of the Exchequer the next and then go on to run banks. What is important is not so much the technical skills – there are hundreds of thousands of very technically able people – nor the managerial skills – there are tens of thousands of able managers as well – but the gift of vision and strategy – there are only a few thousand with that.

One of the reasons why people get stuck in organizations on plateaux is because they repeat successful behaviour which they have learnt in earlier jobs. Now normally this is a very sensible strategy for success but not always so in organizations. Managers who work harder at being technically superb rather than being good managers suddenly find themselves sidelined and out of the mainstream of the promotional ladder. Similarly, managers who spend too much time literally just managing without raising their heads to see where they are going and the context of their jobs will find themselves stuck in their careers.

The diagram below illustrates the concept of the relationship between the major skill sets. You will see that they are present and indeed necessary in all the jobs within the organization but the amount varies.

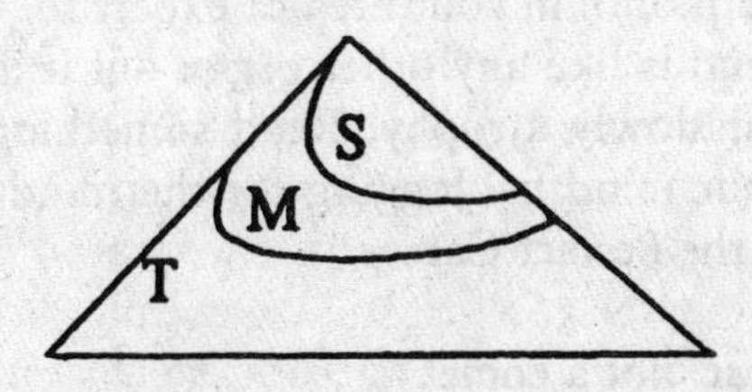

S = Strategic Skills
M = Management Skills
T = Technical Skills

Remember business, like life, is a social activity and you gain more from cooperation than you do from competition and cooperation takes the development of interpersonal skills.

'*I never met a man I did not like.*'
Will Rogers

29. Keep up to date

Once upon a time you could gain a qualification and then say 'I'm qualified'. It was as if learning had finished and then work began – two separate processes. This, however, is no longer the case. Technology is moving at such a pace that qualifications get out of date. In times past it was easy to be a bow maker – it was centuries before the gun was invented – but in today's world you are lucky if your technology stays relevant for more than five years.

Even in the soft sciences like psychology, much has changed in ten years – so it is paramount to keep yourself up to date.

It is suggested that an average person reads just one book a year. Just think what you can achieve by reading one book a month in your area of expertise.

The mind is like any other organ – if it is not used, then it will slowly atrophy. Read something regularly and get your mind fit. Jogging for the mind will make you fit for the Perfect Career.

30. Be a star, not a comet

Comets are spectacular when they are around but hopeless to navigate by since they appear so infrequently. Far more reliable are the stars – always predictable, always there.

Organizations need stability to be successful and they need stable people. It is better to be a star – even a distant one – than put in a spectacular performance on an infrequent basis.

It is much better to be someone who can be relied upon to do something on a regular basis than someone who will do it brilliantly one day but not be there the next. You might achieve fame – more people know about Halley's Comet than about Ursa Minor – but the famous do not get the promotions!! Predictability and consistency in performance are required for the Perfect Career.

'*It takes perspiration and not inspiration to succeed.*'
Dean Sydney Evans

31. Fantasize

'*Imagination is more important than knowledge.*'
Albert Einstein

Everything starts with an idea or desire or wish. Even simple desire like feeling hungry or thirsty. The idea comes and then you do something about it to turn the idea into a reality, to convert a dream into an action. Now why should this operate only with the little things in life – why not the important themes? What do you dare to dream for yourself? What do you aspire to? What are you hungry or thirsty for in career terms?

Questions I ask people in my career seminars include:

1. What would you do if you only had 12 months to live before you were struck down by lightning (and you had visited all the places you ever wanted to and prepared your family for your early demise)?
2. How would you spend the rest of your life, guaranteed at least 20 years of good health, if you inherited £10 million?

3. What one thing would you do if you knew you could not fail?
4. Who would you like to be if you could be anyone in the world (living or dead, male or female, fictional or real)?
5. If you could be any living thing (animal or vegetable, bird or banana, fish or fig tree) what would you be and why?

These are not easy questions to answer if you treat them seriously. They draw your values and aspirations from you and your hopes and your fears, your needs and your wants.

Where do your answers come from? What do they mean? Why have you suggested these things to yourself?

Then come the action questions:

- What are you going to do today to achieve them?
- How can you position yourself to achieve them?
- What resources, qualifications and/or network do you need to achieve them?
- What is stopping you and what are you going to do about it – today?

These questions give you an indication of where the main thrusts in your life should be. Where your heart rather than your head tells you that you should be going. If you're not happy with the direction of your career so far then now is the time to take stock and realize your direction before it is too late.

Wordsworth said that the child is the parent of the adult. In other words, childhood experiences make you the sort of person you are. Career choice does the same. When you leave school there are lots of options open to you but by making choices you later have to live with the implications of those choices.

There is a lovely quote by Quentin Crisp which goes something like this:

> 'It is no good looking after the pigs for 30 years and then deciding to be a ballet dancer, because by then pigs will be your style.'

In other words the earlier you make career decisions in line with your innermost values and desires, the more complete you will be, the more perfect your career.

Now it might not be completely possible to realize your fantasy, but you almost certainly can get close to it. I once had a young city lawyer referred to me because, although he was well qualified and very bright, he was a total disaster at work. Once we had begun working together the reasons were obvious. Talking through the magic questions it became clear that he was a frustrated rock star, his whole life was rock music. Now, at the age of 27 it was a bit late to become a rock star but all was not lost. He now works for the legal department of a major record company specializing in copyright issues. It is usually possible to achieve a fantasy or get pretty close to it but you first have to do some work on yourself.

This exercise is repeated more fully in the section devoted to activities and can be found on page 70.

32. Advice to the redundant

People who are specialists in this area now tell us that on average everyone starting a career in the nineties can expect redundancy to occur at least twice to them during their working life.

By far the most important point to remember is that

it is jobs that become redundant not people. No one can be redundant as a person because everyone can make a contribution and has something of value to give. But faced with redundancy most feel a terrific blow to their ego and self-esteem. It is not uncommon for the individual to feel that he or she has in some way been personally responsible for what has happened. Rather like a road accident where the innocent party says to themselves 'if only I'd not taken that route, or left at that time'. So the person whose job is redundant is similarly self recriminatory – 'Why did I take that job?'

There is also a tendency to self rubbish – 'if I can do it, who would want it?'

If you are sick, you go to a doctor. If you have problems with your teeth, you go to a dentist. If your job has been made redundant, go to a career counsellor or pay for some good outplacement support.

Strange isn't it? You spend years at school and the business of getting a job and managing a career is never really addressed. At this time you need support.

There is very little that a career counsellor can tell you that you can't discover for yourself – eventually. After your 200th CV has failed or your twentieth interview, with that amount of experience you should be getting it right – but it is much better to get it right the first time.

Also, you cannot afford to move into another job that is not right for you so you do need good advice. What is difficult is that doctors' and dentists' services can usually be obtained 'free'. Most people don't think to pay the equivalent of the National Insurance contribution on ensuring they have a healthy career.

Getting a job is a process of being turned down and that is the last thing most people want after they are told by their employer that their services are no longer required. You need support during this period. If you cannot get professional help then join or form a self help group. You will find that you will get far more, and learn far more, from your situation if you work it through with others.

'*Security is the mother of danger and the grandmother of destruction.*'
Thomas Fuller

33. Just do it

'*Many are called but few get up.*'
Oliver Herford

Organizations throughout the world spend thousands of pounds or the equivalent every year getting their managers trained in Time Management. The reason for this is simple – the better you are at this essential skill, then the more productive you are. If organizations are prepared to do this with their money, and organizations are usually more careful about their spending than individuals, it seems highly probable that Time Management in one's personal career is going to be of great benefit.

Time Management covers a host of things but there are at least three principles which are essential and directly relevant to the Perfect Career: overcoming procrastination, getting started and goal setting. The last point is so important we give it a whole section on its own (see page 3).

Everyone procrastinates, especially over the large personal projects like getting a further qualification, getting serious about one's network, writing an article, because they are always things which can be done tomorrow, swept to the side by the trivia of today's chores which cocoon us in the familiar and the less challenging.

After goal and target setting, the important thing is just to get started – JUST DO IT.

Just do something for yourself and your career – now, today. Take your career goals and targets and break them down into discrete and identifiable actions that need to be done and allocate a time to them as to when they need to be achieved. Then JUST DO IT. Do something for yourself – now. It is important to remember that you are the only one who is going to take action on your behalf. You are the only person who is interested in your progress so JUST DO IT – NOW – TODAY.

'*A habit cannot be tossed out of the window; it must be coaxed down the stairs a step at a time.*'
Mark Twain

Here are some Time Management tips and strategies to help you overcome your career procrastination:

- The worst, the first: do the things you dislike the most first then the rest is easy.
- Do it for 15 minutes: give yourself just a quarter of an hour every day to achieve your perfect career.
- Finish what you have started: this is simple and obvious, just finish whatever you start in discrete chunks.
- Do it for 21 days: make a habit of spending time on yourself on a regular basis each day for a period of 21 days. It is said that something has to be done each day for 21 days before it becomes firmly established as a habit.

By far the most important aspect of your career is JUST DO IT for yourself.

'*When a fantasy turns you on, you're obliged to God and nature to start doing it – right away.*'
Stewart Brand

34. Self contracting

Because the relationship between employer and employee is so important it is a legal requirement for there to be a contract of employment which covers such things as job title, hours of work, pay and conditions. What some people find helpful in the area of personal career management is to contract with themselves about what they have to do.

Contracting is helpful because it formalizes a relationship and helps make clear what is required from those who are involved.

On my Career Management Seminars all participants have to contract with themselves about their commitment and behaviour, both on and after the programme. Career work is far too important to have people in the programme who are on it just because it is a softer option than being at work. Making a formal promise to oneself about one's personal behaviour is helpful in showing that one is serious about this special enterprise.

Here is a possible personal contract but you might like to just use it as a guide and develop something for yourself.

DRAFT CAREER CONTRACT:

I recognize and welcome the fact that I am personally

responsible for my own career and the way I conduct myself at work. I understand that personal success lies in doing the best I can with the abilities, skills and experience that I have. I also recognize that nothing is guaranteed or certain.

I contract with myself that as from today I will set myself quantifiable, time specific and realistic career goals which I will review seriously no fewer than _____ times per year.

Furthermore, each goal will be broken down into specific tasks and activities and I am resolved to spend no fewer than ______ minutes per day and ______ hours per week/month in the achievement of these activities. To assist and encourage myself in these activities I will reward and encourage myself regularly and fairly.

My career management is a significant life activity for me and I commit myself to undertake it with the seriousness which it deserves, knowing that I am solely responsible for those aspects of my work and career which are within my direct control.

Signed ....
Date ....

One person I know actually got her partner to witness the document so he had a vested interest in her success.

35. Get the highest qualification you can – as soon as you can

'*Never fear the want of business – a man who qualifies himself well for his calling never fails of employment*'.
Thomas Jefferson

In 1944 a Mr Butler, through his Education Act, made secondary and tertiary education available to all who were able in the UK, irrespective of financial status or class. This means that there are now tens of thousands of graduates qualifying each year. Now you don't need a degree to be successful in business – or even to make Prime Minister (in fact, many entrepreneurs, from founders of airlines to retail empires of electronic goods, left school with minimal qualifications) – but it does help, so do GCSEs and 'A' levels and BTECs. Whilst qualifications are not always necessary to be successful in the job because that takes experience, motivation and commitment, qualifications do give you a ticket in the selection race for the job. In these days of significant unemployment employers are demanding qualifications not always required by the job but just to reduce the number of applicants.

Thus the higher the qualification, the better the ticket for the job race for the really top jobs. Do as well as you can with what you've got, especially if you see yourself working for large corporations. Bureaucracies are always impressed by qualifications so if you are able to add some to your quiver, you would be wise to do so. However, do not get seduced into thinking that qualifications help you to do the job or to succeed, as any junior executive with an MBA will tell you – qualifications help you get there but experience and performance in the job count thereafter.

'*It takes a good brain to resist an education.*'
Max Heinrich Eggert

36. Why do you work?
No, it's not for money – if it were, you would not be reading this book. You want a career and this usually

means less remuneration today for more tomorrow or for more personal satisfaction. If it was just for money no one would be in engineering, catering or the NHS.

So if we do not work for money alone, it is helpful and useful to work out why we work and what motivates us and these are usually one or more of the following:

SECURITY: We want to be safe and in control, for life to have a known predictability and stability. It is not that you do not like variety and flexibility, but that you find ambiguity of circumstances and environments difficult.

AUTONOMY: Here we want to be in control of ourselves, others and jobs. We relish independence and enjoy personal responsibility and are always striving for it.

RECOGNITION: We like the admiration and praise from others for what we do. We discover how good we are and indeed who we are because others tell us. How we stand with others and their view of us, our work and performance is very important to us.

AFFILIATION: This is the need to be with others. Some of us are very social animals.

Once you have realized what motivates you, the other implications become obvious and you would be ill advised to ignore them. It is important that you work in jobs, careers and sectors which will satisfy these motivational needs. A nurse may not be very well rewarded financially for what he or she does, but the satisfaction of knowing you have saved a life must be phenomenal.

A desire for stability would suggest large organizations or the professions would be an ideal environment; autonomy brings about a desire to be entrepreneurial; affiliation points to a team orientation.

37. The four keys for the Perfect Career

To unlock the doors to the Perfect Career you need four very different keys that need to be turned at different times and in different sequences, depending on where you are and what you are doing. You can have three perfect keys and without the fourth you will still find your way to success blocked. You can have all four keys and if you use them in the wrong sequence, you will still find yourself outside in the corridor.

Most people already have one or two of the keys and work hard at turning them in the door and become frustrated when the door remains firmly shut against them.

What are the four keys? They are

- TECHNICAL SKILLS
- MANAGEMENT SKILLS
- STRATEGIC SKILLS
- INTERPERSONAL SKILLS

With a few moments' thought it becomes obvious why abilities in only one or two areas are not sufficient to carry you through. You could be brilliant technically and be good at management, but unless you knew where you were going, anticipated difficulties, sought opportunities and were able to work well with others, your chances of a Perfect Career would be somewhat reduced.

As an exercise you might like to draw your own pie chart reflecting the current status of your skills in each area. Does it looked balanced as in the first figure or does it look more like the second figure, which is the more usual?

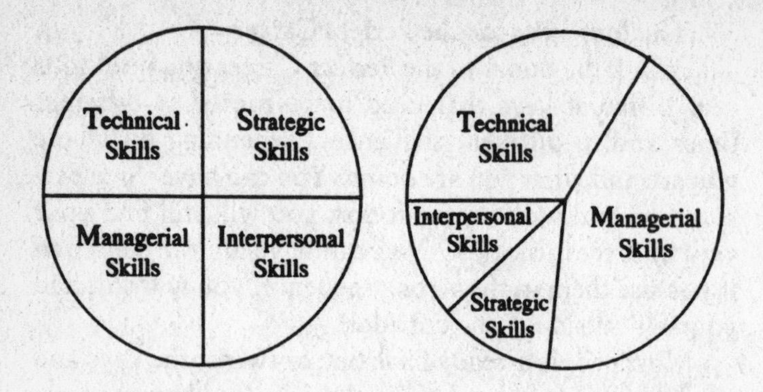

TECHNICAL SKILLS: These are the basic skills for the job covering knowledge of how to do what you have to do. They can include producing a set of accounts, closing a sale, designing a project or writing a programme. In other words, fulfilling the duties and functions of the job descriptions. Whether you are working on the bench as a fitter or sitting at the board table on the top floor, you have to be technically competent.

MANAGERIAL SKILLS: These are how to lead, motivate, direct, delegate, supervise, plan, organize, control, administer, monitor and reward your work and that of others. Notice that it includes your own work, self management, so it is important.

STRATEGIC SKILLS: These are to do with vision, knowing where you are going and what is required to get there. This is understanding the context and *raison d'être* of your work, where it is going and your role within that context. With strategic skills you can see the implications of your work and the options that it presents both your organization and yourself.

INTERPERSONAL SKILLS: These are essentially how to get on with others and how to influence them appropriately. This is often an overlooked area and so it has its own section (see page 25).

If and when your career is blocked and the door to your future is closed, review your four management keys to help you decide where you might profitably concentrate your efforts, energy and resources to achieve your Perfect Career.

38. Dress for success

Have you ever thought why it is that different birds have different coloured plumage or why the same species of fish have the same markings? Have you ever thought why the armed services spend so much money on uniforms or why chefs wear tall hats? Why do we put policemen under funny blue cardboard hats, kings and queens under crowns and clergymen behind plastic dog collars and nuns in black and white habits?

Dress patterns facilitate not only recognition patterns but response patterns too. Walk into a hotel late at night wearing your jeans or your business clothes and see the difference in the response you get from hotel staff. They too are dressed differently – the doorman in a top hat, the receptionist in a uniform, the junior manager in pinstripes and the manager in a suit.

Since we only display about 15 per cent of our actual bodies, the way we cover up and adorn the rest makes a statement about who we are and how we wish or expect to be treated. On the beach or at the sauna we all look the same except some of us insist on wearing expensive watches or tattoos to keep the statement going. Why is it that Prince Charles will wear a ring with his family crest on his little finger and Joe Ordinary will wear one with a sovereign in it on his ring finger?

In the armed services these little differences are organized and standardized. All wear khaki or blue but all you have to do is look at the lapels, shoulders and cuffs to see how high up or down the organization the person is. These tell you whether you initiate the salute, being the junior person, or expect to be saluted.

Now business organizations are no different. There are uniforms and dress codes at all levels. It is not written down anywhere but just look at the intense dress cloning that there is. These are the uniforms of life. Now you can decide how you wish to appear. This is very important because if you don't look like a member of the Executive Club you are not likely to be invited to join it. As an experiment, get in the lift at work and travel up and down a few times and just look at what people are wearing. It is not long before you realize that people on the same floor wear the same things and this goes for accessories as well.

'*When in the boardroom, dress as the directors do.*'
Max A Eggert

It is nonsense to suggest that you get promoted on the basis of how you are dressed. Your sartorial elegance will not be the key to the boardroom but you try getting there in a Burton's suit!! Not even the directors of Burton's wear Burton's suits. They might wear Marks & Spencer underwear but there are not too many M&S suits, or shirts for that matter, in British boardrooms.

At Sun Microsystems – a very large global computer firm – they have a quaint tradition called 'Dress Down Friday' where everyone, except for sales people, can dress casually at work. The idea is that everyone in the firm can remember the very beginnings and keep up the pioneering spirit of the early days in the company when everyone including the founders dressed in jeans and T-shirts. It is a wonderful tradition but guess what the executives wear on Fridays? Designer jeans, very expensive casual shirts and the best in sports shoes. It would seem that no matter where you are in an organization there is always a dress code. Sometimes it is formal (as it used to be at IBM) and sometimes unwritten (but just as rigorous). It is said that Henry Ford fired an executive because his trousers were too tight.

The implications here are obvious – dress for success. Dress as those who are successful in the positions you aspire to. If your company, be it a Bank or a Burger House, insists that you wear a uniform, wear it well but go to work in the clothes that your boss's boss would wear. Whenever you can, look the part.

'*You never get a second chance to make a good first impression.*'

Anon.

CHAPTER 4

Attitude

39. Be positive

Negative people are not promoted. Sales people who rubbish their competitors' product do not achieve sales, employers who malign their bosses or their organizations find themselves candidates for de-selection. Remember, if you run your organization or job down what you are saying to others and yourself about who and what you are?

If you, or the people you choose to associate with, regard work as

- the daily grind
- the rat race
- the funny farm
- the treadmill

it will become just that and your chance of success, however you quantify it, will be minimized.

Positive people appear confident, in control, attractive and they are usually the candidates for organizational recognition and promotion.

It is difficult to be negative and happy at the same time. Yes, of course, there will be difficult and trying times both for yourself and your organization and part of the way through those difficulties will be achieved by being positive.

40. Personal affirmations

One of my favourite quotes is from Henry Ford who said, 'If you think you can or you can't, you're right.'

To a certain extent we are who we tell ourselves we are.

It is all in the head as we are told. We behave in the way we think we should and act according to who we think we are. Like most things this is sometimes helpful and sometimes not so.

We continually have conversations with ourselves inside our heads. Those of you who doubt this are probably thinking 'Do I have conversations with myself?' And it is this inner voice which gives us information about ourselves – who we are and what we are. Sometimes, though, this information is planted there at a very early age by significant adults who are not always correct in their judgement. You will remember that story of the ugly duckling who thought he was just that and presumably acted accordingly until he was told he was a beautiful swan. If you think of yourself, and tell yourself you are just a progress chaser, personnel officer or sales person, it is unlikely that you will make Materials Controller, Human Resources Director or Sales Director.

Junior people act, behave and dress differently from senior people in organizations. If you tell yourself you are a junior person you will think, act, behave, perform and dress accordingly and, mainly because of this, you stay there. If you choose to stay low in the organization, then that is fine but if you wish to move on then affirmations will certainly help.

Now what is interesting about affirmations is that they should be phrased in the present tense as if you are that person already. If you say 'I'm trying to become a Data Processing Manager/Judge/Brigadier,' just think about what you are really saying to yourself. What does your dentist mean when she says 'I'll try not to hurt you'? Also, using the participle or the 'ing' part of the verb means that you're not there yet – rather like that unfortunately British Rail slogan of the eighties, 'We're getting there', to which travellers responded 'Yes, but we want to arrive'. 'I am trying', 'I am becoming' are not helpful statements because you are still in transition, or still on the way to achievement.

It is far better with your affirmations to project yourself into the future – what you want to be expressed in an 'I am a . . .' format. Then repeat your affirmation to yourself on a regular basis.

It is said of one of the present Cabinet ministers that in the 1950s as a young man he wrote on a napkin in a London restaurant '1990 Downing Street'. He has not made it yet – but he is very close.

You might find this difficult to believe, that by telling yourself about yourself you can change your future, in fact change your environment. If you are one of these people then tell yourself, as an experiment, for 21 days that you are a lucky person. Just say it on a regular basis – I am a lucky person. You will be amazed at how lucky you actually become.

There is a cycle of success which flows like this:

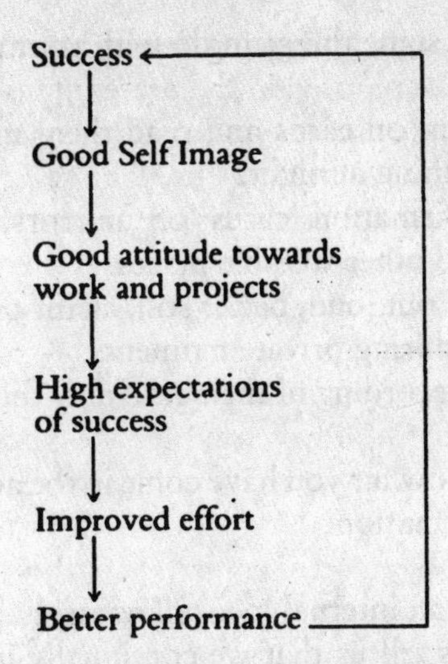

and you can see how this is a loop and once you are in it you can 'spiral up' constantly improving yourself, your work and your situation.

Affirm yourself to become yourself and achieve your career ambitions. Remember Henry Ford: 'If you think you can or you can't, you're right.'

Now you cannot expect affirmations to achieve miracles (although some people with an incurable disease have done just that) or reverse history. It would not be helpful for me to say 'I have a full head of hair' or 'I am President of the United States' since I am fairly thin on top and I was not born in the USA. But I could say, if it was what I wanted, 'I am an attractive person' or 'I am a person of influence in politics'. Clearly, an affirmation will not make me a teenager again nor a champion swimmer since both require me to be under 20, but there are lots of things I want to achieve and affirmations will help.

There is an activity for you to do on affirmations at the end of the book (see page 78).

Here are some things to do with your affirmations:

- Print them on cards and read them morning, noon and last thing at night.
- Place affirmation cards on mirrors, headboards, desks and other suitable places.
- Say them out loud; better still, chant or sing them to yourself during private moments.
- Make a recording of them and play them to yourself regularly.
- Review how far you have come in the achievement of your affirmation.

41. Develop an internal locus of control

Psychologists tell us that we continually interpret what happens to us whether it is good, bad or indifferent and that there is a correlation between our preferred interpretation and our likely level of success. It is called the 'Locus of Control', that is to say, if I was successful I could take the view that it was because I worked hard at achieving the outcome I desired or I could say I was just lucky. In these two interpretations the locus of control changes from internal – I did something – to external – something happened to me.

Undoubtedly there are some very lucky people in this world for whom the wheel of fortune always turns. If in the case of your career, however, you want luck there is usually a long stand. Take control of your life and your career by developing that internal locus of control, decide to manage things for yourself. When things go wrong, and they will, you can blame the situation, the firm, the government, or you can reflect on the situation and what you can do about the future. I did not get the promotion because I do not have the experience, skills, abilities, style, etc. – these are things you can do something constructive about. Now it might make you feel good to blame your failure, difficulty or upset on something external to yourself but it is not helpful.

Some things are obviously beyond your control, such as a quantum leap in technology making your firm go under or the recession meaning fewer people are buying your firm's products, putting your job at risk. These situations cannot be laid at your door but we are in some way responsible for the majority of the events that occur and next time you can approach the situation differently.

42. Visualize

After fantasy comes visualization. Once you know what you want and where you are going, visualize yourself into that position. Here's how.

1. Find a quiet and comfortable place where you know that you are not going to be disturbed.
2. Visualize yourself into the position – what will you be doing, how will you do it, how will people be responding to you?

   What will your manner and style be, how will you look?

   What will you achieve, what will be your results?
3. Use all your senses in your visualization – what will you smell, taste, hear and feel as well as see?
4. Practise visualization regularly and not fewer than three times a week for not less than five minutes a time. (Visualization like anything else takes both practice and time to gain full benefit.)
5. Always make your visualization positive in a situation where you are performing well and at your best.

In sport, top athletes visualize themselves performing at the peak, winning the set, the game or just being first across the line – and it makes all the difference. Remember that top athletes who win, win by very small margins but that is all it takes, just that little bit extra. In developing for yourself the Perfect Career you do not have to be great, just that little bit better than the competition.

'*Where there is no vision, the people perish.*'
Proverbs 29.18

CHAPTER 5

The activities

43. The activities

Knowledge is power and the more information you can have about yourself, the more powerful you become. Achieving the Perfect Career is about knowing what you can do and what you can't; knowing what you would like to do and why. The Perfect Career is one that fits you in terms of your abilities, values, skills and aspirations. The happiest people at work I have met enjoy what they do so much that they are surprised they are paid so much for doing it.

These activities are to help you get to know yourself in career terms and so help you when you have significant career choices to make. A useful analogy is that of a funnel. At the beginning of your career you can go anywhere you want. You can decide what field, what sector, what sort of job. Yes, starting out it is going to be on the bottom of the ladder but it is essentially your choice. No one forces you into the Hotel and Catering trade, Construction, Civil Service, Computing – you choose. So your career funnel is wide and the sides are open as in figure 1.

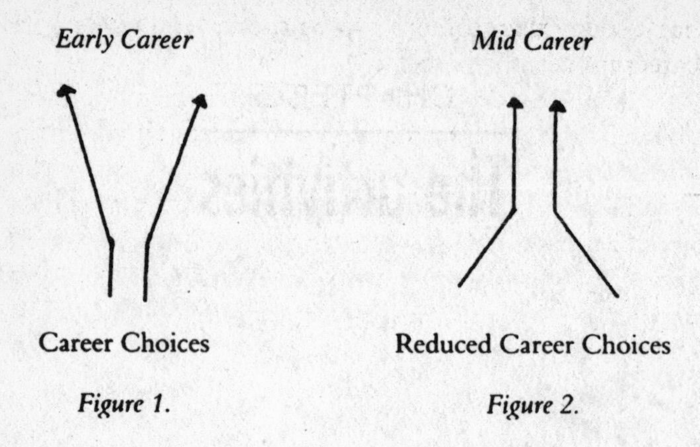

Figure 1. *Figure 2.*

But then, because you have made choices they have career implications and will begin to limit you. You become a victim of your earlier choices. Wordsworth said, 'the child is the father of the man', i.e. early experiences affect later ones. In career terms, your 'career funnel' flips and you have less and less choice because of your earlier choices and age (see Figure 2). It is difficult to become a Foreign Exchange dealer if you have been in shipbroking for five years. It is difficult to get into computing if you have been teaching for ten years and vice versa.

This means make your major career choices as early as possible and also keep taking jobs which push the sides of the funnel outwards to give yourself expanding, rather than contracting, career opportunities. Before accepting a promotion or even applying for a new job – however seductive the salary and benefits – consider and review whether the new position will expand or reduce your career prospects in the long term.

Career changes are difficult and expensive both in terms of salary and promotion prospects. Changing is not impossible. However, since it is easier to break a bad habit today than tomorrow, the sooner you make your career moves, the better.

These activities are to help you discover more about yourself. It is unlikely that you will benefit equally from all the exercises for some will be right for you at this time in your career, others not so useful. Some will be more appropriate for younger people beginning their career, others for those who have decided to make a change or who have been forced into job loss or a career change.

'If you arrive before it's over, you still have a chance.'
Max A Eggert

Activity 1
Values at work
What you value personally and what you value at work are important to both understand and match. It is another way of asking the question 'Why do you work?' or 'What are you working for?'

METHOD

1. From the list below make a card with each value on it (the reverse side of old business cards is ideal for this).
2. Make out five additional cards which say VERY IMPORTANT INDEED, SIGNIFICANT, OK, NOT SIGNIFICANT, NOT IMPORTANT AT ALL, and lay them in a row.
3. Shuffle your cards and then deal out each one under the appropriate classification from Very Important Indeed through to Not Important At All.
4. To ensure a distribution – because some people want

everything – you are only allowed eight cards in every column except for the 'OK' column which has the residue.

5. Then rank the most important first, through to least important for columns Very Important Indeed and Significant.
6. Rank the worst first for columns Not Important At All and Not Significant.

THE LIST OF VALUES

AESTHETICS	– involved in the beauty of things
ADVANCEMENT	– being able to get on and do well
ADVENTURE	– jobs involving risk and daring
AFFILIATION	– enjoying and finding significant friendships at work
ARBITRATION	– being invited to make decisions and judgements
ALTRUISM	– where you can show concern and care for others
ART	– involved in art in any of its forms
AUTHORITY	– the right to direct others because of your organizational status
BENEFACTION	– doing good works for society
CHANGE & VARIETY	– continually changing job content
CHALLENGE	– problem solving and trouble-shooting in difficult situations and circumstances
COMPETITION	– proving your skills and abilities against others
COMMUNITY	– where you can become active in local issues

COMPETENCE	– where you can demonstrate your skills and abilities to a high degree
CREATIVITY	– where you can make novel and new contributions through your original ideas and concepts
CALM	– working in an unrushed and predictable environment
CONTROL	– where you can control your environment
CORDIALITY	– opportunities for you to be warm, friendly and outgoing
CREDIBLE	– opportunity to spend a lot of time thinking; working on the frontiers of knowledge
DANGER	– where there is liability or exposure to harm
DARING	– where there is a requirement for personal courage in difficult situations
DECISIVE	– opportunity to make decisions about options and opportunities
DETAIL WORK	– work that requires precision and attention to detail
EXCITEMENT	– high degree of the unknown in the job where there is novelty and drama
EXHIBITIONISM	– opportunity to shine in front of others
EXPRESSION	– being able to express one's ideas and thoughts in writing or in art
FAST	– environment where things are happening quickly
GLAMOUR	– requiring personal beauty or charm coupled with excitement

GROWTH	– being able to develop personally one's knowledge, experience and skills
INFLUENTIAL	– opportunity to change the view of others
INTELLECTUAL	– recognized as being clever, qualified and a theorist
INDEPENDENT	– being self determined and not dependent on others
LARGE ORGANIZATION	– more than 500 on the staff
SMALL ORGANIZATION	– fewer than 100 on the staff
MORAL FULFILMENT	– personal spiritual satisfaction
PHYSICAL CHALLENGE	– job success requires physical success through bodily strength or speed
PHYSICAL CONDITIONS	– requiring good conditions for work providing personal comfort
PUBLIC CONTACT	– face to face contact with people
PUBLIC PROFILE	– to be recognized in public
RECOGNITION	– to receive positive feedback for good work
SECURITY	– to know that your job and your salary are safe
SOCIAL HOURS	– contractual hours that leave one free to pursue personal interests
STABILITY	– enjoy work which is mainly predictable and unlikely to change
STATUS	– high standing in the organization that brings respect
SUPERVISION	– be in direct control of the work of subordinates

TEAM WORK	– to work as an acknowledged member of a team
TIME INDEPENDENCE	– to be able to work to one's own schedule
TRAVEL CONVENIENCE	– easy to get to and from work
TRAVELLING	– to travel regularly both at home and abroad
WORK ALONE	– to work by yourself rather than be heavily involved in a team
WORK UNDER PRESSURE	– work when there is insufficient time yet work has to be completed

INTERPRETATION

Once you have sorted and ranked the cards, look to see if there are any dominant themes in your selection. How many of these are part of or not part of your job.

How many of these themes will be in your chosen jobs of the future?

Are there any surprises in your selection of cards? Are there any clashes or inconsistencies between the first and last columns?

'No man can climb out beyond the limitations of his own character.'

John, Viscount Marley of Blackburn

Activity 2

Career influences

What have been the major 'pushes and pulls' in your career to date? Who and what has helped you or hindered you to get where you are today?

1. Who has influenced you most in your career?
2. What have been the major turning points in your career?
3. What events have had a significant effect on your career so far?
4. What opportunities have you sought or aspired to at work?
5. Why have you left jobs i.e. what has pushed you out from jobs?
6. What has made certain jobs attractive to you – i.e. what has pulled you into jobs?
7. What do you like about your career so far, and why?
8. What have you disliked about your career so far, and why?
9. What risks have you taken to develop your career? What were the pay-offs?
10. How has your job helped or developed others?

'If at first you don't succeed, try hard work.'
William Feather

Activity 3
What did I learn?
Make a list of the major blocks of time in your life and list down what you learned from them in terms of your career and values. Here is an example:

School
I was good at team events
I can be popular
Some people in power abuse it
Teachers are not always bright or right

1st job
There are some awful jobs about

Doing what I am told is difficult
etc

Activity 4
Exercise for the future[1]
Most of our limits are self-imposed. To create more options one must change beliefs that limit us. Here is an exercise to help you identify things that have changed for you, and things that can change.

Think of your early life and teenage years and on a separate piece of paper complete both parts of each of the following statements:

'I used to believe I couldn't . . . but now I believe that . . .'
'I used to think I was . . . but now I know that I am . . .'
'I used to think that I always should . . . but now I know that it's OK to . . .'
'My greatest fear used to be . . . but now I feel . . .'

In the second part of this exercise, think of your life in the future and complete the following on your sheet of paper:

'In the future I will not be able to:'
'In the future I will be able to:'

Looking back at both sets of information, what kind of trend do you see?

Are you becoming more or less limited?
How does your future compare with your past?

[1] Designed by Dudley Lynch

If you were to rewrite your beliefs to give yourself more choice, what would your new beliefs be? Makes notes for yourself on your sheet of paper.

Activity 5
Magic questions
This is an indirect or fun way of looking at yourself. It is designed to tell you what is important to you and what is not. Some people love this exercise and some hate it. For some it is a very serious way of getting to know themselves, others have used it as a party game at Christmas.

1. What would you do if you had only 12 months to live (and you have visited all the places you would like and have prepared your relatives and friends for your demise and made your peace with your maker)?
2. What would you do if you had £5 million to spend (after you had sorted out your finances, the needs of your family, given some to charity and are in good health)?
3. What would you do if you knew you could not fail?
4. If you could be anyone in the world (Arts, History, Entertainment, Politics, etc) who would you be (you can be male or female, alive or someone from the past, or even someone from literature or film)?
5. If you were an animal, (this includes birds, fish, etc) what would you be and why?

INTERPRETATION

QUESTION 1
The major things of life we sometimes put off because

we can always do them some other time. The question here is why can't I do this now; what is preventing me doing what I really want to do?

QUESTIONS 2 AND 3

Again these tell you what is important to you when all the constraints have been removed. Most of the limitations in life are self limitations and these two questions are a way of confronting them. What jobs or areas should you be working in and at to get close to these areas or functions?

QUESTION 4

Heroes and heroines are very important as role models. This question prompts other questions in this area. Why have you chosen this person? What is it about them that you admire and why? Why do you want to be like them? What is it that they have?

QUESTION 5

This is the same as question 4 but using a different prompt mechanism. In addition, this question gives an indication of how an individual likes to be treated – it says a lot about you if you choose to be a pampered and indulged tabby cat!!

Activity 6

Career anchors

This activity looks at why we work and the satisfaction we gain from our working lives. Once we recognize our anchors then we can develop our career in that direction. We can also select jobs which will allow us to use our anchors.

METHOD

Answer the questions that appear under each of the anchors on a scale of 1 to 5 and by working through this it may become apparent which are the more significant anchors for you by adding your scores in each section.

THE ANCHORS

1. TECHNICAL COMPETENCE ANCHOR:
   - 1.1 I like to be known for my skills
   - 1.2 I enjoy being exceptionally competent in what I do
   - 1.3 I like being an expert in my field
   - 1.4 I avoid work outside my skill competence
   - 1.5 I really enjoy the challenges in my work

2. MANAGERIAL COMPETENCE ANCHOR:
   - 2.1 I enjoy being in charge of things
   - 2.2 I enjoy supervising the working of others
   - 2.3 I like to have things done the way I want them
   - 2.4 I enjoy making decisions for others
   - 2.5 I like to have responsibilities for others

3. SECURITY AND STABILITY ANCHOR:
   - 3.1 I like to stay with one employer for as long as possible
   - 3.2 I do not like to take big risks
   - 3.3 I do not like significant change
   - 3.4 I do not enjoy ambiguous situations
   - 3.5 Security is important to me

4. CREATIVITY:
   - 4.1 I enjoy coming up with new ideas and approaches

4.2 I like being novel and new
4.3 As soon as I can do something I like to move on
4.4 I like my work to be individual
4.5 I like my work to be unique

5. INDEPENDENCE AND AUTONOMY:
5.1 I like to do things my own way
5.2 I find it difficult being directed by others
5.3 I am a better manager than subordinate
5.4 It is important to me to be in control of what I do

Activity 7
Support network
It is often said that it is not what you know but who you know which counts. Managing your own career is difficult when you only have yourself to talk to!! Bearing in mind what has already been said about keeping your long term career aspirations to yourself, it is worthwhile developing a support network. Here are some suggestions.

Someone who knows my industry ______________

Someone who will usually help me ______________

Someone who is honest in their criticism ______________

Someone who knows how to find out things ______________

Someone who challenges me ______________

Someone who helps me through bad news ______________

Someone I can trust ____________

Someone who is good at giving practical advice ____________

Activity 8

Career paths

If you plot your growth, development, progress, salary level and overtime, what sort of pattern emerges and what does it tell you? Or, if you do not have the experience yet, what sort of shape do you want your future career to take to be perfect for you?

Here are some examples with the vertical line representing success and achievement and the horizontal axis time.

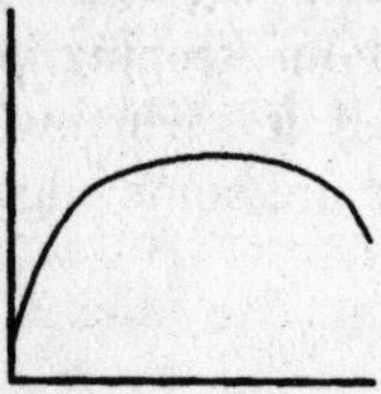

1. Traditional

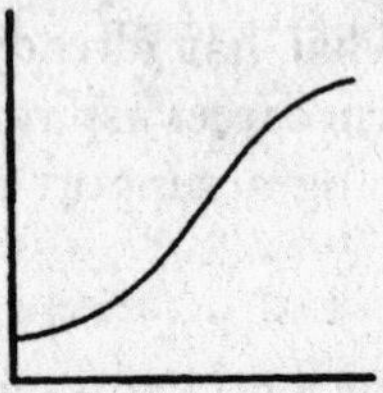

2. American Dream

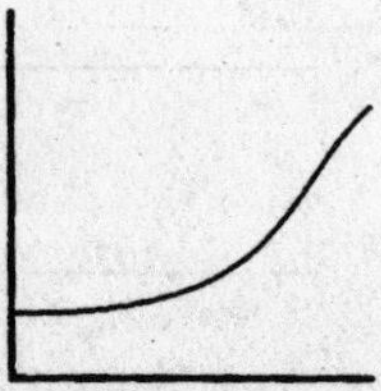

3. Poor start / good finish

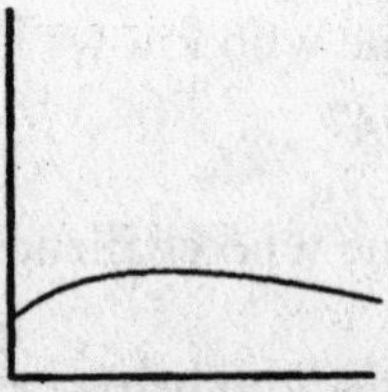

4. Poor start and finish

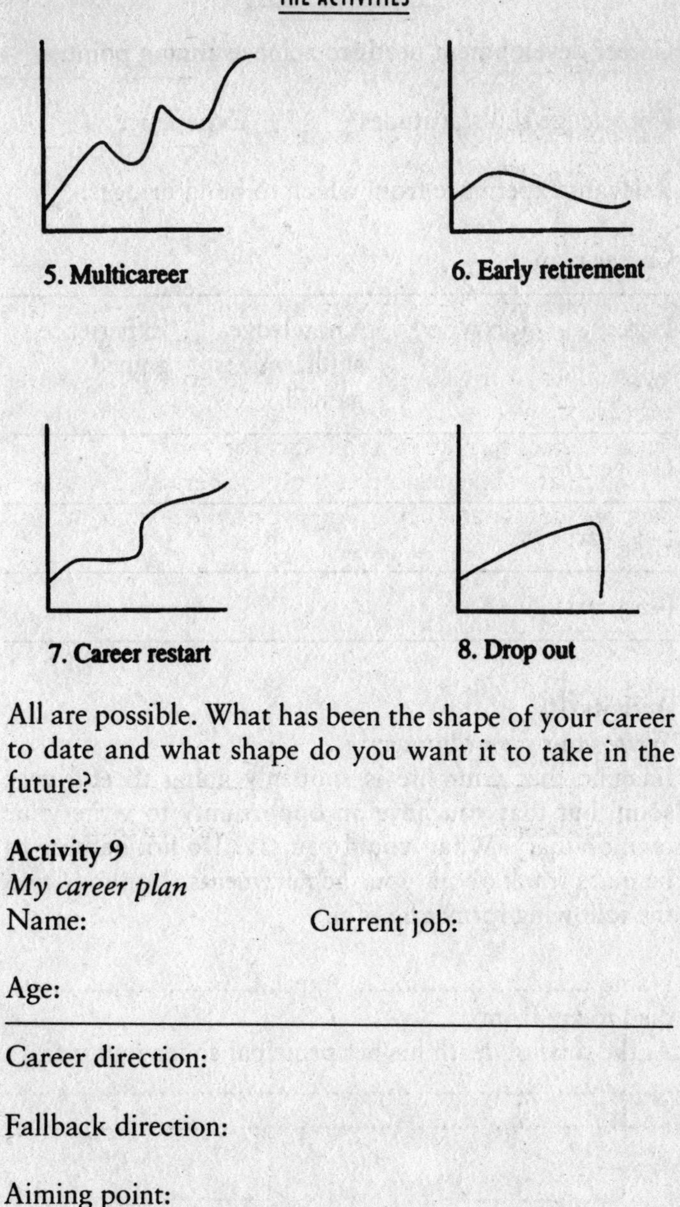

All are possible. What has been the shape of your career to date and what shape do you want it to take in the future?

Activity 9
My career plan
Name: Current job:

Age:

Career direction:

Fallback direction:

Aiming point:

Career development needs to achieve aiming point:

Knowledge/skills/attitudes Experience

Relevant experience from which to build bridges:

Career plan

Dates	Job type	Knowledge, skills, values gained	Experience gained
(+1 year)			
(+3 years)			
(+6 years)			

Activity 10
Write your own obituary[2]
Imagine that your life is suddenly going to end very soon, but that you have an opportunity to write your own obituary. What would you say? Do not hesitate to be quite frank about your achievements. You may find the following format helpful:

Name .... Age ....
died today from ....
At the time of death his/her principal endeavour was
....
....

[2] Based on an exercise by Eric Frank and John Palmer

His/her principal roles included ....

....

He/she always hoped to ....

....

He/she made contributions in the areas of ....

....

....

He/she will be remembered by ....
because ....

....

If you would like to develop this exercise, imagine your obituary appearing in a national newspaper. Use a blank sheet of paper to write what you think would be printed about you. Then use another sheet of paper to write what you would like to be said about you.

Activity 11
Personal achievement review
Someone once said 'Those who cannot remember the past are condemned to repeat it'. This exercise is to help you get to know yourself better. It is always a surprise to me to find how little we know of ourselves and what we have done. This activity is a way of reviewing all that you have done.

METHOD

1. List every achievement you can remember right back to your earliest memory, together with the date. An achievement is something of which you feel proud or something for which you were congratulated by others. It is not necessary to write a huge essay for each achievement, just a few bullet points. Go back

as far as you can remember. Not many of us can remember learning to walk but achievements such as learning to ride a bike and learning to swim would be good examples from early life.

2. If you are in a permanent relationship, share your list with your partner as he or she may be able to remind you of things you have forgotten.
3. Wherever possible, quantify your achievements. So, for example, instead of 'made prefect at school' put 'made one of six prefects out of a form of thirty'. Not just 'promoted' but 'promoted within six months'.
4. When you come on to your achievements at work, then not only quantify them but also make a few notes about the benefits of your achievement to the firm or organization and/or other people.

INTERPRETATION

Classify your achievements into themes. What skill tends to predominate? When are you usually successful? What do your achievements tell you that you should be doing in the future?

Activity 12

Construct your affirmation

Think about what you want to be in the future – what sort of job, what sort of skills or experience will you have and so on. Now develop a short paragraph about yourself.

Here are some examples:

I am a fully qualified accountant.
I am the best accounts manager in the firm.
I am the best trainer in the company.

But your affirmations can also be more extensive and more senior, for example:

> I am a self-motivated and achievement-orientated Finance Director with proven international business development skills.
> I am an international management psychologist who enjoys a professional reputation through my work with blue chip firms and my authorship.
> I am an experienced general manager with an outstanding work track record of maximizing start-up opportunities.

Or they can be directed at specific skills or attributes you wish to develop, for example:

> I am the most creative person in the department.
> I am the best negotiator the firm has.
> I write the best reports in the department.

Affirmations can even help you become the sort of person you wish to be.

> I am an attractive person whose company is sought by others.
> I am a person of value and integrity.
> I am honest and hard working.
> I am healthy and fit.

In this activity list your affirmations.

> Have: One for your eventual job.
> One for skill sets you wish to develop.
> One for personal characteristics you wish to develop.

POSTSCRIPT

Some famous affirmations:

'I know that I am an artist'
Ludwig van Beethoven

'I am the greatest'
Muhammad Ali

'I am by temperament a conquistador'
Sigmund Freud

'I am the Resurrection and the Life'
Jesus Christ

'Captain me am'
Marisiân Eggert (aged 3 years)

Activity 13
Self-image worksheet
For the next few minutes, think about yourself. You have a self-concept, a sort of mental picture of yourself that you carry in your mind's eye. Think about it and write down a few notes. You might find it helpful to discuss it with a close friend or colleague.

Perhaps the following questions will help you form a clearer picture of yourself.

1. What kind of disposition do you have? Is it different at work? At home? With friends? Describe it.
2. How do others react to your personality/disposition? What does your family think about you? What does your boss think? Your best friend?
3. How does the way you dress, talk, walk, listen, etc,

affect others? What type of image do you project in relation to your work? To your social life? To your family?

4. Is the image you project to the world intentional? What self-image would you like? Why?

Activity 14
30 ways to give yourself profile

1. Write an article for your house magazine.
2. Write an article for your professional journal.
3. Write a book.
4. Become a staff representative or a shop steward.
5. Speak at conferences and seminars.
6. Become an expert in something related to your work.
7. Plan profile opportunities for meetings and achieve them.
8. Take an active interest in the same leisure pursuits as your directors or top executives.
9. Organize social events at work.
10. Arrive at work early or leave later than most.
11. Enthuse about your work, never run down your organization, product, service or manager.
12. Play an active part in your professional association.
13. Talk to one new person at work every day.
14. Form or become part of a users' group.
15. Invite experts in your field out to lunch.
16. Write letters to the press.
17. Attend seminars and conferences and always make a comment or ask a sensible question at the end, stating your name and organization.
18. Give genuine thanks and praise to those you admire and those who help you.
19. Take on a project with high profile and network potential.

20. Organize a learning set.
21. See more people face to face rather than use the internal telephone.
22. Organize a charity event.
23. Take part in a charity event and organize the publicity.
24. Write your boss a brief report regularly once a month on what you have achieved and your objective for the next month.
25. Suggest improvements/cost saving ideas on a regular basis.
26. Play golf or tennis with the Chairman or his daughter, son or favourite niece.
27. Ask a senior manager for advice and guidance.
28. Always dress as expensively as you can in the style appropriate to your organization or profession.
29. Ensure your office provides visitors with the best coffee in the organization served out of the best china.
30. Do as much as you can, but with taste, decorum and restraint, to make your office as executive and as well organized as possible.

'Ability without visibility is a disability.'
Max A Eggert

Activity 15

Personally responsible[3]

On a sheet of paper, write what it is – what few critical outcomes – you need to achieve to be successful.

Next, think for a moment about what is preventing you from achieving them, and list these obstacles.

Now ask yourself, 'If I were 100 per cent responsible

[3] After an exercise developed by Michael Higgins

for what I want and do, what would I do differently?'

Activity 16
Perfect career questions

1. What do I want to do with the rest of my life?
2. In what situations do I succeed? Why?
3. What are my specific career goals
   For this month?
   For this year?
   For this decade?
4. What have I learnt today so I can do better tomorrow?
5. What development opportunities are there in this job?
6. How did my boss and his boss get their jobs?
7. Who is the organization man around here and how am I different from that stereotype?
8. How can I give myself profile
   At this meeting?
   During today?
   This month?
   This year?
9. How do people get promoted around here? Why and what for?
10. How can I bend this job
    So I can shine?
    So I can drop my weaknesses and use my strengths?
    So I can develop my skills?
    So I can position myself?
11. Where is the real power in this organization?
12. Who are the power brokers in this organization?
13. What skills do I want to develop
    For this job?
    For my next job?

14. What is the classic career path to get where I want to go
    For this industry?
    For this organization?
15. What is the context of my job? Why does my employer employ me? What is the big picture? What does this mean for my job?
16. What is the market rate for my job?
17. What in my performance makes my boss – happy? – disappointed?
18. How can I make my boss more successful?
19. Who are the blue chip organizations in my chosen field and how can I get into them?
20. What does my boss read professionally and should I read it as well?
21. What do top people in the organization wear?
22. How can I develop a similar interest profile to senior people in my organization?
23. What is the ideal length of time I should spend in this job before moving on?
24. What have I got to do to keep myself professionally up to date
    This week?
    This month?
    This year?
25. If I were to appraise myself, what areas of my performance should I be working on to secure my preferred future?
26. What is the management flavour of the month and what can I do to get up to speed in this topic?
27. What am I doing to keep myself looking good, fit and healthy?
28. Who do I need in my network and what can I do to cultivate colleagues and acquaintances in those areas?

29. What are the success criteria for this job
    For the organization?
    For my boss?
    For myself?
30. How is success measured and quantified in my job
    By me?
    By my boss?
    By the organization?
31. What meetings, clubs or associations will give me maximum profile or networking opportunities for my career direction?
32. What are going to be the future requirements and skills of this job?
33. What skills are required in my next job and how can I develop them now?
34. What professional memberships should I pursue?
35. Who would be the best possible people to advise me on my career?
36. What am I putting off doing to develop my career? Why?
37. What would be my dream
    Job?
    Organization?
    Boss?
    Team?
38. What sort of salary level do I want
    For this job?
    For the future?
39. When should I get into work and when should I leave?
40. What sort of physical environment should I create for myself at work?
41. When should I next review my progress in this job?
42. When would be a good time to review my personal objectives?

43. How can I reward myself for my hard work and my successes?
44. What career errors have I made and
    What have I learnt from them?
    What has been the gift in them?
45. If I were to be promoted tomorrow who in my team would replace me? How can I develop them?
46. Why am I still doing this job?
47. What is the natural job after this one and do I want it?
48. Who are my major competitors for the next promotion and how can I best position myself?
49. What really motivates me? What are my career anchors?
50. What is my preferred management style and how can I best use it?
51. What is my preferred team role and how can I best use it?
52. What should be the landmarks of my career and by when should I achieve them?
53. How can I be more positive
    About myself?
    About my job?
    About my boss?
    About my product or service?
    About my company?
54. What statement am I making through the way I dress for work?
55. What statement am I making by the way I keep my desk, work station, office, plant, complex?
56. Where have I been successful today and why?
57. What is the best way I can reward myself when I achieve my specific goals and targets?
58. How can I keep my network of colleagues up to date with my activities?

59. What am I doing or reading that might be useful to members of my network?
60. With whom am I having difficulty and what can I do to improve my relationship?
61. Are my goals quantified and measurable?
62. Do my goals have realistic dates by which they should be achieved?
63. Is my CV complete and up to date?
64. What newspaper(s) and journal(s) should I read to best support my career aspirations?
65. Where have I taken risks and what has been the pay-off or benefit?
66. If I were to start again in my career, what would I change and why?
67. What have been my significant mistakes and what have I learnt from them?
68. What is the culture of my organization and how well do I fit into it?
69. What have been the major influences on my career?
70. How can I use my time more effectively?
71. How can I improve my job?
72. Am I doing enough to develop
    My presentation skills?
    My communication skills?
    My persuasion skills?
    My negotiation skills?

It is better to wear out than to rust out'.
Richard of Cumberland

21 Reasons for investing in this book

1. You will be more satisfied with yourself.
2. You will be able to work at what you enjoy.
3. You will get more out of your work.
4. You will earn more.
5. You will reach a higher level of achievement.
6. You will maximize your potential.
7. You will be able to work to your own goals and objectives.
8. You will be more confident at work.
9. You will get the recognition you deserve.
10. You will be more secure in yourself.
11. You will be a better manager.
12. You will be a better subordinate.
13. You will be in charge of your life.
14. You will be able to create opportunities for yourself.
15. You will be able to overcome difficulties.
16. You will be able to learn from your errors.
17. You will be better organized.
18. You will be more influential.
19. You will have more business contacts.
20. You will be more empowered.
21. You will not have to wait until you are 50 to realize you are in the wrong job and that it's going to be dif-

ficult to change careers – or 65 and realize you should have done something when you were 50!

'I suggest that the only books that influence us are those for which we are ready, and which have gone a little further down our particular path than we have got ourselves.'

E M Forster

Also Available

PERFECT COMMUNICATIONS

Andrew Leigh and Michael Maynard

Taking for their main topics impact, spoken communication, group communication, honesty, feedback, building relationships, telephone and written communication, creativity and conflict resolution, the authors pilot the reader swiftly and surely through the do's and don'ts and provide all the information necessary to ensure that communications will be perfect whatever the subject and whoever one is communicating with.

£6.99 0 09 941006 0

PERFECT TIME MANAGEMENT

Ted Johns

Managing your time effectively means adding value to everything you do. This book will help you to master the techniques and skills essential to grasping control of your time and your life.

If you can cut down the time you spend meeting people, talking on the 'phone, writing and reading business papers and answering subordinates' questions, you can use the time saved for creative work and the really important elements of your job. Learn how to deal with interruptions, manage the boss and cut down on meetings time – above all, how to minimize paperwork. You'll be amazed how following a few simple guidelines will improve the quality of both your working life and your leisure time.

£6.99 0 09 941004 4

THE PERFECT NEGOTIATION

Gavin Kennedy

The ability to negotiate effectively is a vital skill required in business and everyday situations.

Whether you are negotiating over a business deal, a pay rise, a difference of opinion between manager and staff, or the price of a new house or car, this invaluable book, written by one of Europe's leading experts in negotiation, will help you to get a better deal every time, and avoid costly mistakes.

£6.99 0 09 941016 8

THE PERFECT PRESENTATION

Andrew Leigh and Michael Maynard

Many people are terrified of making a presentation in public, while others are just unsure of how to go about it effectively. But the ability to do it successfully can make all the difference to your personal career, and to the business prospects of your firm. This book provides a sure-fire method based on the 5 P's of Perfect Presentation: Preparation, Purpose, Presence, Passion and Personality. It is an excellent, hands-on guide which takes the reader step by step to success in one of the most important business skills.

£6.99 0 09 941002 8

PERFECT ASSERTIVENESS

Jan Ferguson

Perfect Assertiveness helps you to understand more about assertiveness and its importance as a life skill. The book shows you the difference between assertiveness and aggression, and teaches you to understand more about yourself, the possibilities of change and the potential for improvement in personal, social, family and workplace relationships.

£6.99 0 09 940617 9